THE TURNSPIT DOG

THE
TURNSPIT
DOG

POEMS BY
PAMELA GILLILAN

WOODCUTS BY
CHARLOTTE CORY

BLOODAXE BOOKS

Poems copyright © Pamela Gillilan 1993
Woodcuts copyright © Charlotte Cory 1993

ISBN: 1 85224 144 6

First published 1993 by
Bloodaxe Books Ltd,
P.O. Box 1SN,
Newcastle upon Tyne NE99 1SN.

Bloodaxe Books Ltd acknowledges
the financial assistance of Northern Arts.

LEGAL NOTICE

All rights reserved. No part of this book may be
reproduced, stored in a retrieval system, or
transmitted in any form, or by any means, electronic,
mechanical, photocopying, recording or otherwise,
without prior written permission from Bloodaxe Books Ltd.

Requests to publish work from this book
must be sent to Bloodaxe Books Ltd.

This book was designed by Charlotte Cory, who also drew
Bloodaxe's Viking logo (for Bloodaxe lettering by Gretchen Albrecht).

Cover printing by J. Thomson Colour Printers Ltd, Glasgow, Scotland.

Cover marbling by Charlotte Cory, Dragonfly Press Papers.

Printed in Great Britain by the Alden Press, Oxford.

The creatures are protected
chiefly for their services.
Nature, as yet, is no more
than a useful and necessary
background. It is still
Humanity that counts.

Florence V. Barry,
A Century of Children's Books
(1922)

Does not the Horse and the Ass
carry you and your burthens?
Don't the Ox plough your ground,
the Cow give you milk, the Sheep
cloath your Back, the Dog watch
your House, the Goose find you
in Quills to write with, the Hen
bring Eggs for your Custards and
Puddings and the Cock call you
in the morning?

John Newbery,
History of Goody Two-Shoes
(1765)

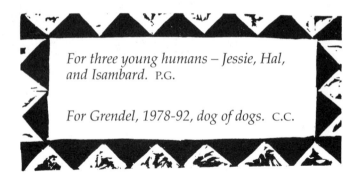

For three young humans – Jessie, Hal, and Isambard. P.G.

For Grendel, 1978-92, dog of dogs. C.C.

ACKNOWLEDGEMENTS

PAMELA GILLILAN: Acknowledgements are due to the editors of the following publications in which some of these poems first appeared: *Another Fourth Poetry Book* and *Another Second Poetry Book* (Oxford University Press, 1981 & 1988), *Freelance Writer, The Green Book, The Honest Ulsterman, New Angles* (Oxford University Press, 1987), *New Poetry 8* (P.E.N., 1982), *New Prospects, Our Earth* (Lancaster Literature Festival, 1981), *Oxford Poetry, Poetry Review, Smoke, Vision On*, and *What on Earth* (Faber, 1989). 'Whisper Who Dares' was broadcast on *Poetry Now* (BBC Radio 3).
My thanks to Drue Heinz of Hawthornden Castle.

CHARLOTTE CORY: I would like to thank Charlie (above) of *The Fiction Magazine* for permission to reprint some of these woodcuts, and Mr Crouch, cab-driver of Wandsworth, who kindly returned the package containing all my artwork for this book after someone, who had better remain nameless, left it in the back of his taxi at King's Cross.

CONTENTS

An Address

 'Now that you're all aboard,'
the Arkangel said, 'There are rules
to be kept. Each of you must expect
a fair share and no more.

The stores should be enough
to last the voyage out – but nothing
to spare. So don't any of you
vegetarians take a wisp of hay

 or a single nut more than you need.
There's plenty of seed for the birds;
they won't burn much energy cooped
under the roof. No flying,

but it's hoped they'll sing.
About the diet of cat-creatures
and other eaters of flesh –
their food is in the hold.

 The scampering and scuffling
will diminish as you sail on.
Disregard my involuntary tears –
their sacrifice is necessary

and not to be seen as punishment
(though all who're stowed below *were*
the third or fourth of their kind
caught trying to slip aboard).

 Your one freedom is to drink;
the rain is clean.
Lastly, try to be quiet.
Roaring and snarling can set up

such fearful tremblings and conversely
a timid bleat may try other passengers
to the limit of their restraint.
Be patient. The flood will bear you up

and I shall watch from the skies
until land is reached. Your duty then
will be to multiply your kind.
But kill or crop or scavenge

for need only, not greed.
I trust you, wild creatures. Now
I'd like a few private words
with the representatives of Man.

Orchids

Early Purples were plentiful; every year
their steeples of close-packed blossom
pushed up amongst the meadow grasses.

I found my rarity, my only Bee,
halfway between Home Farm and Mayhew's
as I loitered along one afternoon.

Wordsworth, Cortez, could hardly have stood
more rooted, have gazed more raptly
at their wide scapes, than I

upon that flower. I rushed to gather
witnesses – mother, brother, aunt;
pulled them down the lane, hurrying,

almost afraid that, unobserved, my marvel
might have changed kingdoms, learned to buzz
and bumble; might have taken wing.

First Fox

A big fox stands in the spring grass,
glossy in the sun, chestnut bright,
plumb centre of the open meadow, a leaf
from a picturebook.

Forepaws delicately nervous,
thick brush on the grass,
he rakes the air for the scent
of the train rushing by.

My first fox,
wiped from my eye
in a moment of train-time.

Leviathan

You can't make whales
make whales.
Chickens don't seem to mind
laying eggs for you;
the patient cow
conceives at the squirt of a syringe;
shoals of fry
will populate concrete ponds –
but whales cannot be handled
contained
farmed
made familiar like dolphins or lions
herded like pigs or sheep.
Their procreation is their own affair
their milk for their own young.
Only in death does man
find them valuable.

None left alive,
their monumental bones
will stand stripped in museums,
their pictures wonderful on the page
at W in a child's alphabet,
like D for dodo
H for humanity.

Animal, Vegetable

Feathered war galleon, the old turkey –
wings stiff, tail spread – would launch
gobbling towards us across the yard.
Rage bubbled in his throat, his wattles
like some inner organ repellently misplaced
dangled that dangerous red
that sent us scuttling home.

Today, skirting a bed of nettles,
cautioned against touching by their
wattle-like cascades of green,
I thought of that turkey and his kin.
For all their choler they've been overcome,
never now lord it over farmyards
but pass their days gregariously
between walls, eating their way
towards heavy-breasted ripeness,
weaned from territorial pride
and robbed of wrath.

Plot

Bramble
shoots up
reaches
grows heavy
bows down,
knuckles
fresh surface
makes roots
makes loops

grows heavy
bows down
drops roots
lifts loops
with calm
tenacity
walk in
takes
over.

Bitterns

(for Anne Spillard)

The first heavy raindrops
starred the windscreen dust.
We stopped by a fieldgate,
wound the windows down. An owl's thin cry
came from a laneside tree

and birdcalls reached us from far away
across water, notes pure and round
as if cupped in hollow glass, but not
the almost-fabled sound we'd come

to listen for. Instead, we stayed to look.
Beyond the low lands that now sprang clear,
now sank to teeming darkness, ranked clouds,
built high and wide, exchanged their fire.

Horizons echoed with axeblows of sound,
drumrolls, growling reverberations.
The bitterns, even in the lulls, held their peace.
They in their marshy reeds beyond the meadows,

we in the rain-washed car, were dwarfed
by noise and brilliance – split-second
rivulets of light streaking to earth,
the extravagant striking of arcs.

Suddenly – Ah!, we breathed, Ah!…

The whole width of the sky was revealed,
a lucent sheeted roof tight as drumskin.
Apricot and flickering white, cast
as if by gigantic smokeless flares,

held us second after vivid second
as inarticulate as those hushed birds.

Roundabout

It's the ostrich again
with his striding legs,
urgent naked neck, reins
slack by the saddle.

Few want to ride an ostrich.
There are dappled horses
and giant shiny-painted cockerels
all making the same journey

round and round. Watch them
rushing past as regular
as rent-day and the day
to put the rubbish out
and late-night shopping day
and empty-saddled Sunday.

Balloon – GMBZH

Early-evening strollers look, hesitate,
gather in a ragged semicircle.
The arena's a green slope that rises
into symmetry – the steadfast embrace
of Bath's Royal Crescent.

Tethered to a purple truck
and to the hands of helpers
a mutable pear-shape striped
in segments of petunia and buttercup
bounces to treetop height.

Then down almost to the grass
before she blows again, lifts,
her basket crammed with riders
getting the feel of it. I count eight,
and two babies are handed up

for a brief bound and drop.
Sunlight slants through swarms
of midges. In fluid formations
they move like motes, loyally bobbing
as if on invisible reins.

Requiem

The spider wove out across the room.
Four pairs of co-ordinated rapid legs
silently bore along his blob of a body
a finger-width above the carpet.

A dropped cottonreel
halted him in mid-rush.
He poised to assess the danger;
reassured, rushed on.

The ginger cat
raised an eyebrow, pricked an ear,
attentively observed his darting course
and as he coasted near
she bent her head and gathered up
the spider. Her mouth
for a moment was fringed
with brittle waving legs.
And then, one gulp,
she swallowed down
the little bit of protein.

Fly

As if lathering his thin elbowed legs –
first the rear pair, then the mid,
lastly the fore, a brindled fly
cleanses himself drily,
poised on a leaf.

His eyes, tense as pebbles,
give back no light, brown globes
dull as dung. Yet they see all ways
at once, a mosaic of sights
set to catch chances of harm.

Thought does not hobble him.
Faster than I can raise my hand
he's gone as if a spring propelled him,
needing no friend to cry
Look behind you!

17

Houseguests

Winter cleaning discovers butterflies.
You see first the downy undersides
of their clamped-together wings.
Some are keeled over, dry leaf-shapes
for the broom to take.

Today I disturbed one by the skirting
under a chest of drawers. It faltered awake,
freed itself from a drag of dust,
began to taxi tremulously out
across the carpet and then settled,
wings closed again, and was lost
in the browns of the pattern.

A dangerous camouflage. I took it up,
added it to my ward of sleepers.
They rest in an air-holed box,
waiting for Spring, sometimes stirring
to crawl a millimetre or two –
though not by the twitch of an antenna
do they welcome each new presence.

Double Glazing

No way in – yet there he is,
single creature hatched
from the risky chrysalis
into a shadeless prison.

Freedom would seem to be upward
through the sandwiched air.
He climbs the sheer face,
slips, drops, steadies himself

by a flick of wings;
climbs again, drops; again.
Alighting he'd not disturb
a daisy petal – and never will,

will touch nothing that grows.
The windowed scene (trees,
silent river) lies beyond his vision.
Now in noon's magnified heat

six filament legs still scurry,
two feelers flail and swivel,
thread-fine arcs searching
for something beyond the smoothness

that wastes his short-straw life.
No mating flight for him – only
a slowing struggle against barriers
that look like light.

February

Desperately the first man-beings
must have watched bare twigs
for a new breaking of green,
afraid that a kind season

might not befall again.
They'd have found gods then
out of their need
to propitiate and entreat

for if there were no asking
there might be nothing given –
no warmth, no replenishment.
As the light came earlier

each following day, bringing
only a bone-cold dawn
how their faith must have faltered;
how they must have stood silent,

hungry, under skeleton boughs,
willing the leaves to come.

Hellebore

She entered the meadow
though a gap in the thorn
clambering up the bank
into an open width
where grassblades shone
in the cold sunlight
windflexed sickles
uniformly curved.

Where the crook of the hedge
gave shelter the green plant
blossomed, every part green
from stem to cup
and strong, a flower
of underworld from darkness
where no bud quickens
into white and yellow.

False, that tale
of sweetscented asphodel –
how much more seductive
these sombre pendent heads
with their strangeness
their look of latency
as if into great profundity
their roots reach down.

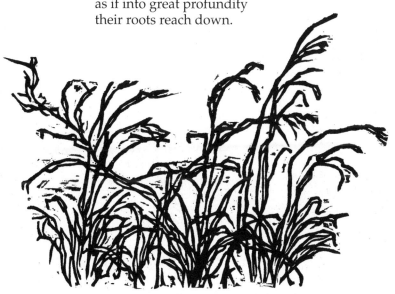

Kermoal

Currents more fluid
than water follow contours
of chimney and wall.

From stones and roof-tiles
wind-coaxed music keens, shrill
as from a bowed saw.

Grassblades, willow, fir,
apple boughs, all in movement
toss on the cold air.

Will Spring never come?
Magnolia petals fall, edged
brown from the wind's bite.

Apples

This year I left the apples on the tree
for birds to pick at for their autumn food,
not even gathering one of them for me.

Watching them probe and balance I could see
that I had done the very thing I should.
This year I left the apples on the tree,

took none for keeping, but birds feeding free
seemed to be something sensible and good.
Not even gathering one of them for me

from all the scarlet crop that brilliantly
shone against yellow leaves and lichened wood
this year I left the apples on the tree.

December; still I watch the two or three
left red as baubles for a Christmas mood,
not even gathering one of them for me.

For once, it's true, I could more easily
forego them – they were small, not very good
this year. I left the apples on the tree
not even gathering one of them for me.

Listen

The rustling thickets of summer
do not change visibly nor alter
the pitch of their whispering, yet all
together, as a flight of birds inexplicably
wheeling – a thousand changing course
without discernable leadership – so the leaves
at some moment between light and night
change the content of their respiration,
withdraw benefaction. In sickrooms
tulips and roses are lifted in vases
to unpeopled corridors, until morning.

Is it the rising sun that then
triggers the reversal?
You may stand at every dawn beneath trees
straining to understand but you'll hear
no sigh, no click of a switch
between taking and giving.

But neither do you hear across oceans
a keening from once-inviolate forests
as the green growth of centuries vanishes
into thin and thinner air.

Leavings
(for F.S.)

The clover's still here, left in the milkbottle,
bunched up like a powderpuff, delicate fan
of stems through the glass like a man o' war's tentacles,
bright as green trefoils still fresh in the lawn.

I stand by the windowsill breathing the sweetness –
already less sweet, there's a hint of decay
and all the peripheral florets, I notice,
are papery brown and beginning to die.

Two days is the lifespan of this small arrangement,
each white richly-scented leguminous head,
and after tomorrow your flowers in the dustbin
will rot among teabags and remnants of bread.

But though you went early, your brief weekend over,
you stayed in my memory; not brother or lover,
just picker and smeller and buncher of clover.
And who could ask more? Even love's not for ever.

Maytime

In New York State they watch for the dogwood
to flower, glancing aside as they drive
along Parkway and Freeway for first sight
of its white clusters. In London there's lilac
in bud and kerbside plane trees slow to leaf
while in Cornish woods the curling bluebells
fade like old men's eyes and rhododendrons
burst lavishly from foils of evergreen.

Looked-for signs; but this harsh Spring
inexorable weather-streams still swirl
above our heads. Vast pourings, they
rush to fill or drain, strive to make level
the heights and shallows of air's oceans –
courses that cannot be dammed
or channelled or oiled smooth.
On the last day of this year's May

it's so cold that primroses bloom on,
so wet that seeds rot in the ground, so windy
that orchard blossom has been shaken down
too soon. We search for reasons – distant battles,
forest fires, volcanic dust. We know Earth's
changes make our weather; yet how feebly
seek to prevent what may come – May's buds
scorched dry; a heat to be feared.

Fishing for Roach

Ten, twelve years old, we never wondered
by what genesis they'd come, to swim
numerously in the landlocked
farm pond where horses came to drink.

Feet of waterboatmen puckered the brown water.
Rings grew from the nudging mouths of fish
and moorhens dragged their rippling
arrowhead wakes, rocking the duckweed's

green platelets. We sat on the bank
watching the float till the water's chill
interlaced August's heat; the ash, the elms,
cast teatime shadows. Time to go.

We shouldered our shilling canes, rolled up
our tuppenny lengths of line, careful
with the barbed hook that caught so cruelly;
took the day's catch home to show.

More tomorrow; every fine day we fished.

A Walk in Another County

The church tower was of unsmiling flint
and flints lay scattered where we walked –
blunt shapes, various and eccentric.
We weighed them in our hands.
They were sponges once, someone said.

Working boats curve in to the island harbours
of the Aegean, framed up like pergolas
to carry a harvest of moist brown pouches –
sea-creatures that, set to rot, will yield
a residue of thirsty honeycomb, something to buy
under lamplit trees from peddlers stationed
with full trays, like flagsellers; something
small and weightless to fly home with.

Flints have a rind of chalky patina,
a dark core harder than steel.
Surged to the surface they lie
like lumpish roots. Yet a blow
can wake them to sharpness,
to lapidary sheen. In that countryside
their split planes face out from barns
and cottages, arcane but commonplace –
long-used resource for killing-blades,
tinderboxes, stubborn walls.

In my granite house a month later
the flints are in my dream.
Tall geese in a bare field stoop to peck,
then lift their long throats, to swallow
the stony tubers that lie along the furrows,
changed and unchanging, like a gorgon's tears.

The Road

On a day dappled with bright cumulus
I thought myself distanced enough
by years and the season to trace
his November journey.

Butterflies, warm air, the claytips
shining white beyond green hedges –
none of these had enriched
that solitary walk.

He'd have stepped quickly,
shrugged into his sheepskin coat.
I know the swing of his thighs,
how his feet touched ground

as he strode through the last
hours of his life, saying goodbye
to the world, light, time –
himself.
                    Yes, there was something

shared after – a meal, a conversation,
or how would I know of the road and how far
he walked, and who it was (chance-met)
who drove him home.

Wonderful Bird

The postcard he's sent me
is of a pelican, posed
on a wide rail against
blues of sky and water.

Sleek plumage, spread feet
clawtipped as bats' wings are
and the teased grain
of salt-weathered wood –

all unnaturally clear.
The camera has focussed an eye
sharper than any human's
to bring him close.

The pelican's own eye
is round and knowing.
His beak rests on the curve
of his breast, ready to lift,

carve his flight-path.
The postcard might have been
of a hummingbird, or a bird
of Paradise, but this

is what he chose – a hunter,
primitive and confident.
Remember, it says.
Remember.

POSTCARD

Cat through a Window

Panther-black she leaps, turns
in the air, tosses her toy to be caught
in upstretched paws, tossed again.

Her tail is a fifth limb, she's so whole
bodily and in intent, so fluidly agile.
At half the garden's distance

her play is a dance in silhouette
against a green ground, her prey
no more than a bundled shape

already inert. Is it for a purpose
she's been teasing, to unloose
the tenderising juices of terror

in her winged or whiskered catch?
At last she's still, crouched; only
her head tilts as her jaws lever.

Then she stands and without a glance around
stalks off to a warm room, and loving hands
and soft milk for her salty thirst.

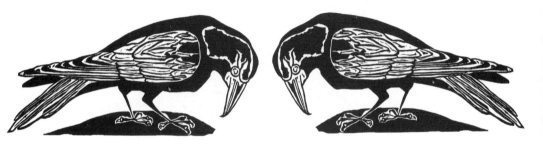

Better than People

We were in the kitchen
washing dishes. Suddenly she stung.
What do you want to get pregnant for?
Childbirth's nothing but blood and shit
and cats are better than people any day.

I know her story now. Cats do have virtues.
They stay where they're comfortable;
thrive on human love; conceive in pure lust –
mostly breed strong and perfect.
Fastidiously with barbed useful tongues
they cleanse their newly-born of blood and shit,
and when the warm nest cools they fill it up again.
No fuss, no sorrowing.

For Kerrin

In Rhodes
there is a garden full of cats
viewed from a bridge parapet,
like a sunken stage,
a long garden full of arid beds
like graves.
Perhaps graves?
An old man tends it,
dragging a few flowers from the dust.

And all among the regimented plots
ranged like a plan of Manhattan
or a field of war graves
(could they be war graves?)
the old cats lie on their flanks,
the little dusty kittens
and half-grown cats on stalky legs
prance and play.

They live in a closed world.
They don't look up
at us, gazing down.

L'après-midi d'un chaton

(at Arboras)

He's from England, the little grey cat.
The family brought him through Customs –
singing, so they said, to cover
the sound of muffled mewing.

A French cat now, a castle cat,
his purr is a warm round noise,
small in the vaulted kitchen.
He plays alone, soft-pawed
across widths of coral-coloured stone,
leaps up the tower's shallow stairs,
whirls down again, skimming
the splayed footworn treads
like a ball of dust in a draught,
and out into the sunlight, chasing lizards.

Crouched among flowers, he turns
his golden eyes to watch
a wide-winged butterfly, scrambles
in mock-fright into peach tree branches;
ignores us idling away the afternoon
on the shaded terrace – wineflushed, content,
and alien to him as any humans, anywhere.

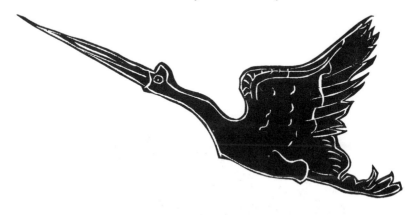

Cat and Man

He found her, limp as a dead creature,
carried her indoors. One ruined eye,
a taut sphere red as garnet,
headlamped her cleft forehead.

She was a young cat then, and she lived.
For three healing days she lay motionless
and then crept secretly down the stairs
to the garden two floors below

relearning her way with halved sight.
Soon there were mice, even birds, again
between her claws. She catches nothing now.
She snores, and her barrel-belly swings

as she trots greedily to her filled bowl.
But sometimes she'll still prance,
feinting at shadows, or patting
at dropped pens or cottonreels,

skidding them across the floor.
And, even when she's asleep, if I crumple
a waste sheet of paper she at once opens
her eye, half-rises as if to run in chase

as she used to – his game with her. He'd throw
towards the basket and she'd leap, catch,
toss the rustling ball, then sit alert
watching the hand that would throw again.

Tuned to that sound she'd answer it
at mine or any hand, though for her the man
is no more remembered than her vanished kittens.
These days I often tear the papers,

drop them, a rough confetti, into the bin.
But in both throwing and not throwing
I acknowledge him, as in all
my actions and abstentions.

Riddle

You could slake a small thirst
from my cup or take
my smooth worrybead
of a seed and cast up
slow centuries of growth. I'm planned
to outlast you, stand high
above you. Make me, raw stuff
for your saws, into stairs,
beams, doors, shelves, rough
firewood, fine chairs. I am air
for your breath, I am loam
for growth. You, who need Earth
for your home, must revere, must spare
me; there will be no birth,
only a dwindling to death without
me and my kind. We are beacons;
we flare to guide, to warn.
Watch our green burning – while we
live you come to no harm.

Plane Tree at Aghia Triada

Zeus, himself Cretan born, made three sons
with Europa, sired the first under the ever green
plane tree. He put on horns and hoof
(though why he thought she'd less desire man's
shape than bull's who can explain?)
for his wooing, so mild in windblown scarf

of hillside flowers that she was not afraid.
Take three leaves, bear three sons – a package offer.
The childless wife from Luton reaches, climbs,
hopes her wish won't be disallowed; she's made
proviso that she wants at least one daughter,
for surely even gods move with the times.

North Wind in Crete

Down the swirling road in the taverna
they play the same tape again and again.
I order moussaka; she shakes her head.
I shy from the offered alternative –
bull's testicles, grilled; instead
eat fleshy tomatoes soaked in oil.

Beyond the dusty yard, their rhizomes
half unburied along a crumbling ditch,
the canes' tall quills dangerously bow
and recover, bow and recover.
A goat's cry thins into streaming air.

The taverna is open as a barn,
doors wide for the lion April
rushing through.

March into April: Rethymnon

Bending like Gamma (upper case) we struggle
across the airport's rainswept tarmac.
The north wind whips surf from a steely sea,
ravages the rows of tamarisk.

Two cold days and then a new wind
pushes across the mountains from Africa,
warm but no less powerful, carrying
flights of stinging sand. The waves

have not the strength to break.
Each swell, dinted like hammered metal,
falls short beneath offshore gusts
that override the shingle's drag.

Inland, mimosas toss green-feathered limbs;
splinters from flailing roadside canes
confuse the air like dragonflies.
We leave as the island heats and dries.

Cloud-parodies of snowy Ida build
in a blue sky. Newcomers step from the plane
confident of sunshine, towards trees
motionless as flowers under glass.

Counting Sheep

The leader forced its woolly bulk through a gap
in a greened-over stone hedge, shook itself
like a dog – and became one, smoothhaired, lean, brown –
then sprouted a pair of webbed wings
and took off in an erratic dragon-flight.

Fascinated by these metamorphoses
I lost sight of the rest of the flock
until I thought of the dipping-trough.
I got three safely through. They sank,
surfaced, scrambled, and miserably emerged.

The fourth, struggling unduly, gasped
and gave birth as she swam; the fifth plunged
contemptuously – a hairy, sceptical goat.
It was when the man in an office suit,
holding tight to a smart briefcase,

strode to the brink, eager for immersion,
that I switched on the light and the bedside
radio, and fell fast asleep.

To My Father

(23 August 1891 to 7 January 1967)

Yesterday, the day before your birthday,
reaching between leaves for the brown figs
amongst the many still hard and green
I had the sense of a watcher poised

a shadow-length away. Was *he* here?
Had I, out of longing, hauled him here?
But less likely a lover's ghost to visit
than a father's, drawn back

by a multiple and less requited love.
That you'd held me newborn in your arms,
flicked my milk-teeth loose, bandaged
a hundred wounds, had counted for nothing

when, adolescent, I pressed for freedom,
rebelled against your curfews,
ducked away from the hand
that would have smoothed my hair.

I wonder – was it an invisible
insect-stir in the bushes by the path?
Or, if a presence, was it you, father,
come to watch me gathering the figs?

I used to wrap them in soft paper,
bed them in a box to send to you,
fourth week in August, the first ripe ones,
to celebrate your birth.

Relinquishment

He left the house,
the garden and the roses,
sold all his years
to someone who might prune
and bud; who equally might
let canker in, and riot.

A hundred miles away
with twine and knife
again he made a garden
where in June he bunched
roses for every jar and vase,
while still as many buds
loaded the bushes.

He'd learnt, however old,
to start afresh.
He'd learnt relinquishment,
that life's a loan.
His bone-ash feeds
the churchyard rosebed
as he'd wished it should.

His widow took me there
and wept, her eyes
cast to the soil,
while the wind drank
from scented heads
and quiet petals fell.

Passing San Michele

In an English garden I saw a tall stone monument
inscribed to the memory of a dog –
Venom, beloved and faithful friend...

Mother, Father, you each have no more
than a line in a crematorium list;

lover, not even that, no name lettered
in coloured ink for casual eyes to catch.

Last week as the vaporetto butted the landing
at San Michele I might have stepped ashore

to savour the certainty of marble and cypresses
on that island walled from the water,

where gondolas come heaped with flowers
but I remembered the uneasy tenure

of Venice's dead, lifted after a lease
of private years for gregarious reburial

while that Victorian dog lies alone
until the sky falls, beneath his name –
though griffon or Great Dane who knows now?

The Turnspit Dog

In the museum of a country town
they'd posed him, stuffed, as if he ran
perpetually in his cylinder,
a ratty creature, rough of fur,
shortlegged by design. Just once
I saw him but I've often since
thought of his task – his treadmill paws
unresting during roasting hours.
When, dinner cooked, they let him out
could he then doglike run about
or did he prance, like marking time,
until they hoisted him again
to turn a wheel, as water would,
or wind? But he was flesh and blood.

Dilemma

The dilemma is a fabled creature
and differs from the unicorn
in having never less
than two horns.

It lurks behind decisions,
threatening constantly,
using the tactics of attrition.
If you don't look this beast in the eye
it proliferates in a twinkling
and surrounds you.

Its multiple proddings
can wound the psyche
and weaken the will.
I would tell you, if I knew,
how to avoid encounter with it
but the truth is…

A Way Out

'Come into my quandary,' said the dilemma,
ushering me into a private garden
enclosed by high walls on all four sides.
Paths criss-crossed the grass
leading to many exits.

The creature spun me round three times.
'Be off now,' it said,
'You can't stay here for ever.
Just choose a door – they all
lead somewhere.'

The Dogs

In a country that had been terrorised
and overrun, the carnage suddenly stopped.
People crept from hiding, incredulous, cautious,
and began to walk in the streets.

But always on the far pavement, like dreamcreatures,
stood the moonfaced large dogs of that land.
They had been given no shelter, but their fierce eyes
and flowing pelts had saved some of them

from death and cold. Their flanks were taut,
remembering the gunbutt, the shone boots.
They would never again approach an offered hand
or come to a man's heel.

Charlotte Square

This is a city restless as any city.
Between parallel channels where traffic
wells and gushes, in daytime spring tides
and night-time's neap, is a grassed island
foottracked between street and street.

Here the town dogs are brought to run
twig in mouth or soberly leashed.
For them, fine ashlar facades,
the symmetry of fanlights,
even the scuffed grass and fallen leaves,
have no significance. Meanings,
for them, thread the wind.

A grey soft-pelted dog races towards
the man's addictive scent, drops a stone
at his feet. The man throws again.
Each gives what he can, striving to please
across boundaries; the owner and the other
to whom nothing can belong.

Looking

As she walked she'd be looking down,
expecting to find something of value
dropped onto the grass. So much there –
thousands of silver rings torn
from fizzing cans; white half-burned
cigarettes; chocolate-bar wrappings
with a sheen like real gold.

New Year's Day: the pasteboard carcase
of a spent rocket, a champagne cork,
a scrap of paper, deep blue, shining up
like a gentian. The neighbourhood dogs
ran past her, circled and squatted.
She gathered nothing worse than mud
on her shoes, nothing better than a glove
she set carefully on a railing.

The months brought no prizes.
Then, one afternoon, scuffing her way
amongst drifts of dry leaves,
she looked up for a long moment.
The avenue of beeches held the last
of their fullness against the haze
of a larkspur sky. She saw how the dogs
scampered between the boles, burrowing
and nosing into the russet mass,
heads down, finding nothing.

Bodmin Ponies

Night-bold the ponies clop down the empty
village street, find fenceless rights of way,
push against garden gates,
press u-prints into winter lawns.
They amble onto flowerbeds, crop
the moonlit leaves of vegetables.

We wake in the dark to their sounds –
the strike and scrape of hooves,
exhalations, amicable jostlings
as they sidle for warmth along the house-wall,
cluster beneath our window – narrow heads,
round rumps, long flowing tails.

By day they keep to the moorland,
distant, cautious, as if remembering
the town's yearly use of them, the roundup
for summer rodeo. One at a time,
affronted by the weight of incubus,
they sashay into the ring,

plunge, twist, rear, kick, try every trick
until each clinging Jack-the-lad's pitched down,
rolls clear, slaps at his jeans
and swaggers off, to cheers or catcalls.
The pony shakes itself calm, strolls aside,
bends to taste the arena's meadowgrass.

Lighting the Fire
(at Hawthornden – for Caryl Phillips)

New flames, three luminous founts –
at first three voices, single, uncertain –
now hum in unison.

On the other side of the room
the clock whispers, using carefully
the strength of its battery heart.

I must sit quietly, let it come,
the word that says weather, that says wind,
that tells how the windowglass softens
the rage outdoors (as, rainstained,
it filters daylight), gentles the roar
so that the room's in balance,
a hive of soft sounds.
But I need only look outside
to bring the distant sighing close,
translate it into fury,
feel the world rocking.

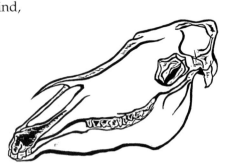

A Rainbow and a Cuckoo's Song
(W.H. Davies: 'A Great Time')

Words that come crowding are banal and trite
at that first glimpse. My mind says fairyland;
says filigree; says delicate; says bride-white;
then lace, perfection, sparkle, diamond…
Picturebook scene, it brings a childish joy –
framed in the window, painted while I slept
and, sun already up, soon to be drawn away
and upward in invisible vapours sipped
by a thirsty sky. If every frost-spun point
needles the consciousness, with its certainties
of change and loss, how deeply piercing is the sight
of this crystal dust defining a thousand trees.
Conjoined, like arc and bird, there may not come
April and snow again, this side the tomb.
(Snow at Hawthornden, 9 April 1988)

Shadows

The first giant caterpillar
was brindled like tortoiseshell,
as big as a cat. Green blood
stained my shoe when I stamped it dead.

The second, oily white,
its segments almost translucent,
scrabbled at speed acoss the floor.
But I was faster – and woke,
gasping with revulsion.

What had my dreamfeet burst apart?
Whether dark fibrous moth
or stained-glass butterfly,
the creatures would have spread monstrous wings
between me and the sun.
Or so I feared in my dream,
stamping, stamping.

Beetles

They scuttle from us, belly-to-the-ground,
run under anything that offers a crevice
or a shadow, in fear we'll strike down
with a broomhead, stamp with a shoe, for no reason
other than that we don't like their looks.

I remember a whirling panic one night
when a maybug flew in through the car window,
ricocheted crazily around in the dark.
Why were we afraid?

We lift ladybirds from grass stems,
perch them on children's hands – scarabs,
cracker-ring gems. They'll cling, but soon,
hinging the lacquered red, they stretch
narrower wings of black-veined gauze, fly away.
Friends, not plague however many hatch –
and most summers they're uncountable.

But it's a long time since a big black beetle
crossed my path. Encased in funereal coachwork,
advancing those stiff antler-jaws
he's been seen as a prophet of rain,
an old-wives' omen of doom.

The poet Lucanus, a protege of Nero's,
fell out of favour and was commanded
to slit his own veins. Lucanus Cervus,
the stag beetle, is under a slower sentence
as the ancient woods, with their spread
of nourishing rot, are lost.

Who'll save him? He's not fashioned
to enlist our sympathy; rather, his shape
arouses squeamishness. I'm one of the many
who'd draw back from touching him –
and from his soft grub that shares a role
with toadstool, crow, and vulture,
all those that clean up, and make way.

Iron Age
(On Solsbury Hill)

We left the car halfway up the rise,
approached on foot along the lane.
Wild arum leaves were dustless, glossy,
the flowerhoods still underground.

Ruched in new green a line of hawthorns
fended the wind from us until, climbing
the earthwork's slope, we broke
into bareness, a wide stage, closeturfed,

spattered with April daisies, no bush or tree
standing against the wind, no boundary
but the edge, the drop to encircling farmland –
variegated, functional, the forest's

tamed successor. Now this height is the wilder;
unploughed ages lie deep over the scars
of hearths where the first ironmasters
made tools to ease their living and, in fear,

death's sharp instruments. In the Easter sunshine
we walked slowly, at ease, as if the Earth were safe.

Fragments

The lawn he once made so fine
sifting the earth for planting
is rosetted with dandelion leaves,
lanterned with their seedheads,
invaded by coarse couch and onion-grass.

In the house are empty walls,
the paintings gathered over the years
gone, only the thief knows where.

There's a sketch in the margin
of a museum catalogue – a detail
set down for remembering.

I found writings in a folder;
his thoughts.

Of all the words that passed between us
few can be brought to mind. Once he said
All I want from life is to be happy…
And afterwards denied it.

The Lady and the Unicorn

Her purity deserves the finery she wears,
the small innocent fauna that surround her,
the flowers fresh and perfect
sprouting from her woollen field.

A thousand shivering sheep released
into the winds of several Springs
and many unremembered men,
hands and backbones irrevocably bent,
sight sacrificed by rushlight,
have made, strand by strand
with much skilled patience, this tribute
to her quality; honouring also
another patience, the unicorn's.

He would not presume, like Europa's bull,
to offer her his back and a rewarding
dizzy gallop towards experience. No.
His eyes upon her are bland, docile.

Almost he disowns the ridiculous pale spiral
set like an unlit candle above his mild brow.
He does not seek to kindle her maiden curiosity;
perhaps he knows nothing will.
Virginity is her profession;
she's an expert at it.

Whisper Who Dares

Carefully chosen, charming and fun,
the nursery's new wallpaper
bides its time until he's kissed,
warm for the night, alone.

Along the picture-rail thin snakes
begin to writhe. Fierce eyes stare out
from flowers and foliage. A menagerie
comes to life in the night-lit room.

Lions are shaking their yellow wigs
ready to spring, a wild rush
of teeth and talons, unless he watches.
A million scorpions, a trillion spiders,

lurk in coverts of viridian leaves,
scuttle without sound if he looks away.
He recites Gentle Jesus, hands together,
eyes closed while the voice protects him.

He tells neither God nor parent
about the haunted walls, nor about
the midnight shape that hangs on the door,
batlike, hunched, trailing a tasselled tail.

Tartary
(a song of childhood)

Bring to a rolling boil. Marinade. Fold in.
The recipes had pictures interleaved –
brown slabs of meat in moats of gravy,
puddings turretted like sandcastles.
My skills – and permissions – went no further
than tinted fondants and peppermint creams –
a sifting and blending of powdery sugar
with egg-white, cooking essences,
and, mysteriously, Cream of Tartar.

Was this a skimming drawn at evening
from the milk of mares when
after the day's thunderous riding
the Tartars sat encircling their smoky fires,
domestically still, the gleam
of their eyes in brown eclipse
as they nodded in the warmth?

And jellies. My mother said
they came from hooves; why not the hooves
of Tartar horses? What happened at the last
to those brave-chested steeds
whose feet of polished horn flashed bright
as they flew in tireless gallop under vast
empty skies? Did their carcasses
litter the steppes, leg-bones axed and bloody,
while mounds of hooves were shovelled
into the holds of old steamers bound
for jelly refineries on Thames- or Mersey-side?

No answer between the red boards of Mrs Beeton,
or the dark blue of Walter de la Mare –
her trustworthy prose, his song of lordship.
Gold; flaunting peacocks; mandolines.
And a bed of ivory. Quinqueremes
sailed through our guiltless minds
laden with prisoned apes,
immaculate tusks.

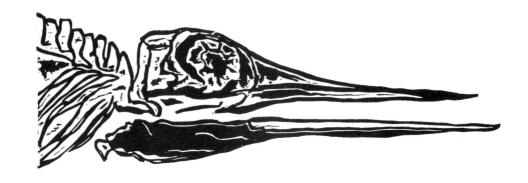

Something of Importance

The cloth is like a harbour
crowded with ships. Its weave
is whiter than seafoam; dishes ride
like galleons, cargoed with delicacies:
roast meats, whole fishes spiced
and glazed, puddings laced with wine,

fruit mounded upon comports
of gilt and crested porcelain.
Brocade and velvet cushions
lie puffed on the woodland grass
and there the ladies stand, shaded
by swathed and feathered hats,

their skirts a rippling fall, the rosettes
of their slippers peeping. The gentlemen
are no less grand, satin-breeched and caped,
all at attention as from her carriage
the young queen steps down,
is seated to grace the feast.

While she sits so may they,
and they may eat and drink no longer
than the lasting of her appetite.
They must play the games she chooses –
tag, hide-and-seek, blind man's buff –
and seem to enjoy them. They must listen

to birdsong with her, recognise the flowers.
She points to a solitary white calyx
that bows and trembles above the grass
on a stem like silver hair. No one can name it.
We shall ask the professors, she cries,
Let a sentry guard the blossom.

In the silence of their wake he's left
under the trees, tall country boy
in epauletted scarlet. Another will come
to relieve him at the watch's end,
and so through all the white flower's life,
its seeding and shrivelling, and on

through the forest's fall of leaves
once and then many times. But no summer
bring such a flower again; the earth
in the grove is too hard, pounded
beneath the sentries' boots. They stamp
as they come on watch, stamp as they go.

The queen does not picnic now – she's old
and she rides in her closed coach. One day,
midwinter, through the glass she sees a flash
of scarlet beneath the snowy boughs. A man
in this raw wilderness! The gale assaults
the carriage; cold reams her bones.

She does not ask what duty holds him,
but sends post-haste a brazier of coals,
orders a shelter to be built.
The guardhouse will grow to a garrison
far from any frontier. Generations of men
will spend their lives there, guarding something.

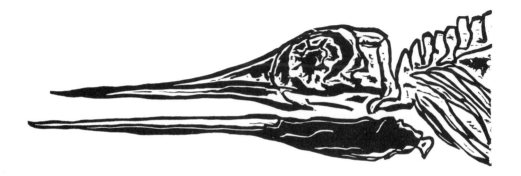

Mission

The Ark, tightly cargoed, leaps into space.
Earth's last men watch its first few years –
the encapsuled future (human-seed, the germ
of leafgreen synthesisors) seeking a harbour

many lifetimes distant. After this, no more chances.
The watchers' faith foresees a concise
though unrehearsable sequence of arrival:
first the plants, then embryos uncurling

in new-made air. But thrown off course
by an unimagined chance, the ship betrays
its conceivers. Purposeless, a blind mote,
it sails on past planet Ararat.